# Zoom In, Zoom Out

Written by Amy Leask

Photos by Octavian Ciubotariu   Illustrations by Jane Li

Dedicated to our moms and dads, who taught us
to see and to think.

International Standard Book Number: 978-1-927425-20-6

Author: Amy Leask
Photography: Octavian Ciubotariu
Illustration: Jane Li
Design: Ami Moore
Editor, Publisher: Ben Zimmer

Zoom In, Zoom Out first edition published by:
Red T Media,
300 Bronte St. S.
Milton, Ont., Canada  L9T 1Y8
905.864.1858
1.877.872.4619
www.RedTKids.com

These two little critters
like to have a look around,
gathering bits of information
on some things that might astound.

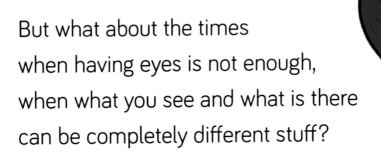

But what about the times
when having eyes is not enough,
when what you see and what is there
can be completely different stuff?

And what about a camera
and the photos it will take?
Can you trust what's in the pictures,
or is that a big mistake?

So...zoom in, zoom out.
We're about to take a peek
at whether eyes and cameras
give the answers that we seek.

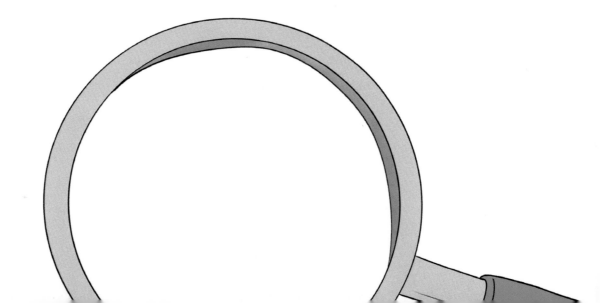

# What is that?

Zoom in, zoom out.
Take a tour around your head!
Can you trust your eyes to tell
about the stuffy on your bed?

I'll have this one figured out quick as a wink.

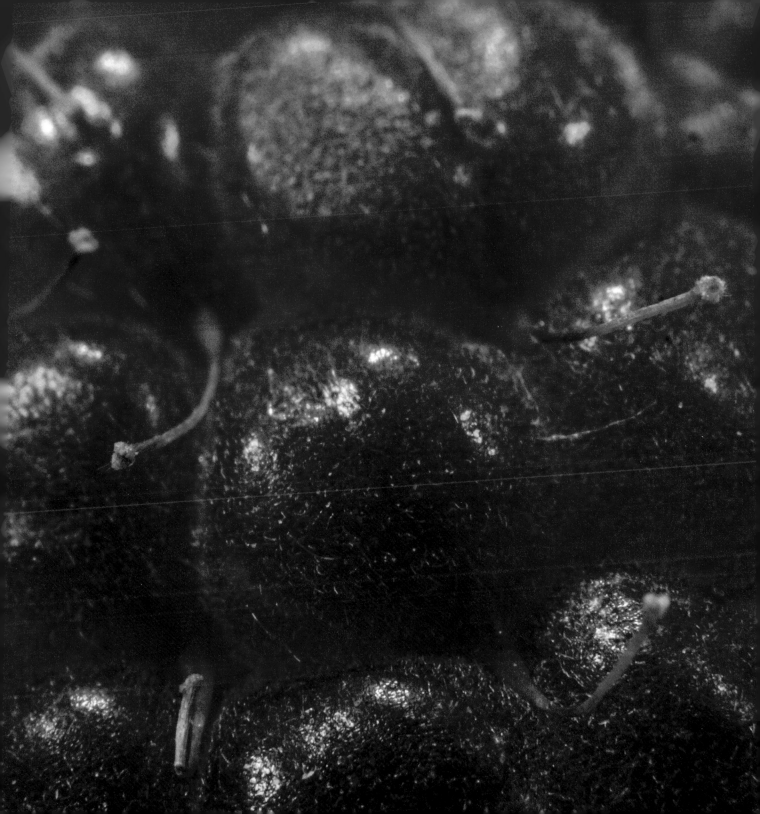

Zoom in, zoom out.
This is so extraordinary!
Can you trust your eyes to tell
about a plump and juicy berry?

This one will take some focus.

Zoom in, zoom out.

Let your eager eyeballs linger.

Can you trust your eyes to warn

about the thing that pokes your finger?

Zoom in, zoom out.

Look as closely as you're able.

Can you trust your eyes to tell you

what's for dinner, on the table?

I can't believe my lens!

Zoom in, zoom out.

Wild and wooly thing, it ain't.

Can you trust your eyes to see

what helps you play with blobs of paint?

I wonder what that could be...

Zoom in, zoom out.

Maybe look a little more.

Can you trust your eyes to tell you

what is rolling 'round the floor?

I "shutter" to think what that might be...

Zoom in, zoom out.

It's a thing beyond belief!

Can you trust your eyes to tell you

what is oozin' 'cross the leaf?

Does my eye deceive me?

Zoom in, zoom out.

Are you seeking something sweet?

Can you trust your eyes to tell

about a warm and gooey treat?

If our eyeballs can be tricky
and our cameras sometimes fool us,
then what can thinkers turn to
when surroundings try to school us?

A brain can come in handy
when we're not sure what we're seeing.
It can help us sort through pictures
so that things will start agreeing.

Our brains are cute and squishy
and a lovely shade of pink,
but they also come in handy
when we really need to think.

So...zoom in, zoom out.

Give your eyeballs room to putter.

Let your camera have a turn,

and leave your brain to sort the clutter.